TOUR of LIFE

Tour of Life
is dedicated to

Janet
God's gift, my partner

Congregations with whom I've served
First Christian Church (Disciples of Christ), Henry, Illinois
First Christian Church (Disciples of Christ), Mandeville, Louisiana
Heart of the Rockies Christian Church (Disciples of Christ), Fort Collins, Colorado

Colleagues whose faith shapes my own
Joan Dennehy & Scott Hardin-Nieri

Orville L. Wright
My father, whose ministry planted the seeds of my ministry

TOUR of LIFE

A Baptism and Confirmation Journey

Jeff Wright

CHALICE
PRESS

ST. LOUIS, MISSOURI

Bible quotations, unless otherwise noted, are from the *New Revised Standard Version Bible*, copyright 1989, Division of Christian Education of the National Council of the Churches of Christ in the United States of America. Used by permission. All rights reserved.

Cover and interior design: Elizabeth Wright

Visit Chalice Press on the World Wide Web at
www.chalicepress.com

10 9 8 7 6 5 4 3 2 1   10   11   12   13   14   15   16

EPDF: 978-08272-36639

Library of Congress Cataloging–in–Publication Data

Wright, Jeff (Jeffrey M.), 1950-
Tour of life : a baptism and confirmation journey / Jeff Wright. — 1st ed.
   p. cm.
Includes bibliographical references.
ISBN 978-0-8272-3661-5 (pbk.)
1. Christian life—Textbooks. I. Title. II. Title: Baptism and confirmation journey.
BV4511.W75 2010
248.4—dc22   2010034901

Printed in the United States of America

CONTENTS

INTRODUCTION

Faith Is Caught, Then Taught: The Thinking Behind Tour of Life

A Baptism and Confirmation Experience That Models a Life of Faith and Discipleship

Go therefore and make disciples of all nations, baptizing them in the name of the Father and of the Son and of the Holy Spirit, and teaching them to obey everything that I have commanded you.

Matthew 28:19–20a

We were seated around a table in the church's kitchen—eight young candidates for baptism and I, their pastor—sharing soft drinks, a bag of potato chips, and conversation about what it means to follow Jesus. Halfway through the class, I looked at the youth and thought to myself, "There's one of us even more bored than the rest: *Me*." This wasn't the impression of the Christian life that I wanted to leave in our youth.

Later, the incongruity struck me. In our baptism/confirmation classes we too often describe the adventure of discipleship—living with Jesus in the world—while seated around a table in the church. I want our youth to experience the challenge and joy of following Jesus in the world, where we fulfill our calling as disciples.

Tour of Life is built around the premise that the truths and practices of the Christian life are more enthusiastically embraced as they are "caught," not simply taught. For example, on Easter morning in our church, children are invited to crawl under the communion table from behind—as if into the tomb—and to emerge out the front, as if the stone had been rolled away. Even our youngest are encouraged to participate, sharing in the joy of resurrection long before they can understand and articulate it.

By observing others and "practicing" life for themselves, children begin to walk, count, and pray long before they understand the significance of these behaviors. In the same way, believers of any age are more likely to grow in their faith by sharing life alongside more mature disciples than by reading a book about discipleship or attending a class. *Tour of Life* leads participants on a journey through the seasons of life. They are invited to experience God's hand at work in everyday experiences. For more details about how this Tour is structured, see the "Overview of the Tour" or talk with your group's Tour Guide.

First the Experience, Then the Faith

In the prologue to his gospel, John writes, "And the Word became flesh and lived among us,...full of grace and truth" (Jn. 1:14). Jesus' disciples were led to the startling conclusion that the fullness of God was revealed in the words, works, and relationships of Jesus. This expansive claim lies at the heart of our faith as

Christians. "Emmanuel," they said of Jesus, meaning "God with us." Most religions teach that, by way of a list of things to believe and say and do, people may work their way through to God in heaven or to a comparable concept of salvation. Christianity announces the good news that God has made a way through to us here on earth. Christianity announces that God "lived among us" as a carpenter/ teacher and experienced life as we know it in all of its ups and downs—full of grace and truth.

Our teachings about God and what it means to be human, then, are not only spiritual truths. They are also concrete, practical realities that God reveals across racial, ethnic, cultural, and historical boundaries. We encounter these realities in the midst of life's joyful mysteries and terrible losses: the birth of a child, the touch of a loved one, the betrayal of a friend, the contradictions of the human heart, the costs and rewards of daily work, the challenges of living in community with others. These truths are written into the fabric of creation, which, when discovered and embraced, help us live life to its fullest.

After Jesus' death and resurrection, the disciples didn't set out to begin a new religion. They simply shared what they had experienced of God in Jesus. They set out to follow Jesus in their everyday lives: trusting in the things that Jesus had told them, doing the things that he had done, experiencing his continuing presence. They were called followers of "the Way" (Acts 9:2) because they practiced a way of living they had discovered in Jesus. They followed a way of forgiveness, generosity, justice, humility, compassion, and hope, empowered by their experience of the living Christ.

We declare to you what…we have seen with our eyes, what we have looked at and touched with our hands, concerning the word of life…
1 John 1:1

The Experience of Resurrection

Although Jesus had tried to prepare his disciples for his death and resurrection, they responded with shock and disbelief when the risen Lord greeted them that first Easter morning. Their lives were transformed as each told the others of their experiences: "The tomb is empty." "He has appeared to Simon." "I have seen the Lord." "We recognized him as he broke the bread."

That tiny band of believers began to turn the world upside down—or right side up. They embraced resurrection as a concrete and universal reality in this life. Old hurts were healed. Broken relationships were mended. Physical illnesses were cured. People turned from their sins and lived lives of integrity, justice, and service. The walls dividing people and cultures were torn down, as tired ways of seeing and shaping the world gave way to new ways of being and doing. They discovered that death doesn't have the last word in this life or the next. People were attracted to Christianity, not first of all because of its beliefs and rituals, but by the disciples' behavior. *Jesus' followers practiced resurrection*, living lives of love, compassion, and courage in the face of danger.

As the community grew, Christians turned to the Scriptures and prayer in order to reflect on their experiences. They gathered to give thanks to God, to celebrate what was happening in their lives, and to teach "the Way" to others. Writings and liturgies emerged to carry the memory of Jesus' life, death, and resurrection and to help the community recognize God's Spirit at work in the world. Rules were written and traditions emerged to shape the community's life. Doctrines

Then they told what had happened on the road, and how he had been made known to them in the breaking of the bread.
Luke 24:35

were commonly embraced to preserve revealed truths. The disciples organized a mission of preaching and service to witness to the experience of resurrection throughout the world. They became *church*.

But all this came later—comes later for each of us as we, the community of Jesus' followers, seek to make sense of our experience. First, we encounter the experience of God's love and power—then, we find our faith in God.

Church consultant Kennon Callahan[1] reminds Christians that John 3:16 does not begin, "For God so loved the *church*...," but rather, "For God so loved the *world*..." The church has been entrusted with an extraordinary message. It is good news about life in its concrete realities: its joys and sorrows; unexpected surprises and terrible losses; seeming dead ends and unexpected second chances; its strange and wonderful mysteries; and its incredible fierceness, beauty, and diversity. In the midst of it *all*—not just in the church, not just for Christians—God is revealing God's self and inviting persons into a relationship of trust marked by a life of discipleship.

Tour of Life invites participants to discover God's redeeming presence in the world. With the encouragement of a Tour Guide spurring them on, the group will explore a life of discipleship as it is empowered by God's Spirit, supported by the church, and lived daily—from birth to death to life anew, again and again. Together, tour participants will make the joyful discovery that God's kingdom is coming and God's will is being done just as we pray, "on earth as it is in heaven."

Jeff Wright
Epiphany 2010

---

[1]Used by permission of Kennon L. Callahan, *The Future That Has Come* (San Francisco: Jossey-Bass, 2002).

ITINERARY

Tour Destinations

New Birth: *Becoming a disciple of Jesus is like starting life over again.*

Disciples and mentors meet at a hospital birthing center, where they observe the newborns. Then they gather in the hospital's cafeteria or classroom where, in pairs, mentors and disciples introduce themselves and talk about the connections between our first birth, as children, and our new birth as people of faith. The tour guide may give an overview of the tour and talk about the longing in all of us, at times, to begin a new life.

School: *Disciples learn together with Jesus.*

The group travels to a school's foreign language classroom. The classroom's teacher may be asked to welcome the group and say a few words in that language (then to translate!). The tour guide speaks about how new Christians essentially are learning a new language. Several words are discussed, especially as they relate to our everyday life: *sin, forgiveness, atonement, salvation,* and *sanctification,* among others. In pairs, mentors and disciples discuss their experiences of learning and what it means to become disciples (pupils) of Jesus.

Work: *Disciples get a job loving God and others.*

Participants share in a service project: raking the yard of an elderly person, preparing the meal at a local soup kitchen, working on a Habitat for Humanity building site. At the project location, disciples and mentors gather to discuss what they enjoy doing, what they do well, and how they are learning to do these things even better. Mentors are invited to talk about their vocations and how their work is a means of expressing their faith. The tour guide helps disciples see that our job as Christians is to put the dreams, strengths, and talents God has given us to work in our daily lives.

Walking in the Spirit: *Disciples experience God's presence everywhere.*

After an introduction, participants experience the ancient practice of praying through a labyrinth. Disciples and mentors share their experience of the labyrinth and talk about the rhythm of a Christian life: moving inward in relationship with God and moving outward in service to others. The tour guide introduces the Holy Spirit and both the gifts and the fruit of the Spirit. Resources of faith are discussed, such as prayer as conversation with God, and the Bible as revelation

and encouragement. The group explores what Jesus means when, in John 15, he says, "Abide in me."

Meal Time: *Disciples are fed at the Lord's table.*

The group returns to the church building, where a meal is served around the communion table. Participants are encouraged to connect the Lord's table in worship to the family dinner table in our homes. Families give thanks to God for food and life around both tables, sharing the day's events, listening to each other's stories, remembering the past, and looking to the future. They are fed physically at both tables! Each time Christians gather around the Lord's table, they are reminded that all of life is a banquet God spreads before them. God invites them, like Christ, to take life, bless it, break it, and share it with others.

Play: *Disciples enjoy God's creation and their relationships.*

The group is invited to relax and play. Following a few games either outdoors or inside, the tour guide invites the group to observe the nature of play and the importance of rules that impart structure and meaning to play (and life). Sabbath and the Ten Commandments are God's gifts to the community of faith, setting boundaries so that the community may rest, relax, enjoy, and share life to the fullest.

Death and Resurrection: *Disciples face death with courage and hope.*

The group travels to a funeral home, where the conversation turns to death and resurrection. The funeral director may be asked to speak briefly about death and grief. In pairs, mentors and disciples discuss their experiences of death and their understanding of resurrection. Participants are encouraged to identify ways in which God brings new life out of old in this life (forgiveness in relationships, second chances, the healing of broken bones, and reconciliation between nations). This new life extends to the eternal life that God gives as a gift. The tour guide may be prepared to talk about the two most important experiences of resurrection in the history of God's people: the exodus (from a life of harsh slavery to a life of freedom, accountability, and justice), and Jesus' resurrection from the dead.

Church: *Disciples gather to celebrate and prepare.*

Back in the church building, participants talk about their experiences of *church* (both positive and negative). In pairs, disciples and mentors explore the meaning and significance of the body of Christ and the need to regularly gather as believers. Christians gather to remember and share God's love; to seek God's presence and celebrate God's action on behalf of the world; to learn together about God, life, community, and self; and to prepare to anticipate and share God's presence in the world. The tour guide invites disciples and mentors to experience how the church's rituals and practices nurture trust in God's loving presence and the church's mission in the world.

Tour
Destinations
for
All Travelers

NEW BIRTH

1

Becoming a Disciple of Jesus Is Like Starting Life Over Again

"No one can see the kingdom of God without being born from above." (Jn. 3:3)

In the Bible, we read about Nicodemus, a Jewish leader, who came to Jesus in the dark of night to ask him about living for God. Jesus said that it's like starting life all over. You must be born again, Jesus said—born from above by the Spirit of God (Jn. 3:3). Nicodemus didn't understand what Jesus meant. "I'm a grown man," he said to Jesus. "How can I enter my mother's womb again?" Jesus must have smiled. He was using a figure of speech to help Nicodemus understand that giving one's life to God means learning a new way to live.

"Like newborn infants, long for the pure, spiritual milk, so that by it you may grow into salvation." 1 Peter 2:2

Think of a baby just born to its parents. An infant is completely dependent on others for everything it needs: food, clothing, shelter, warmth, touch, and love. A newborn doesn't know how to walk. It doesn't know how to talk. In ways just as concrete and practical, we need God and others to help us grow in a life of discipleship.

When we become Jesus' disciples, he teaches us how to walk in ways that bring joy to us and the world around us. Jesus teaches us a new language: the language of faith, hope, and love. Jesus teaches us how to build healthy relationships, how to care for others, stand up for ourselves, speak the truth, and hold to what we know God wants for us and for the world.

First, the milk, the basics of faith, Paul writes in his first letter to the new Christians in Corinth (1 Cor. 3:2). Then comes the meat. *Deciding to trust and follow Jesus is like starting life over again.*

Trip Journal

New Birth

Becoming a disciple of Jesus is like starting life over again.

> "No one can see the kingdom of God without being born from above." (Jn. 3:3)

Group Discussion

What must it be like to be a baby?

What do babies need in order to thrive?

How is becoming a Christian like being born again?

Mentors and Disciples in Pairs

Beginning something new can be fun and scary at the same time. Write down your feelings as you waited for everyone to arrive and the tour to begin. Are you scared, happy, curious, or do you have any other feelings?

When you meet a new person, in what ways can you help start a relationship?

How can we begin a relationship with Jesus?

Read Colossians 3:12–17 aloud together.

Babies can't dress themselves. As newborn Christians, Jesus wants to "clothe" us with special qualities. Paul lists many of these qualities in his letter to the Christians in Colossae.

How do these qualities of life compare and differ from the way you are living now? To the ways people around you behave? (Write your ideas here. Be prepared to share with the group one of the ideas you shared as disciple and mentor.)

If you could take a picture of one thing you saw or experienced at this stop along the tour, what would it be?

To Read on Your Own Later

When, like the apostle Peter, we profess that Jesus is the Christ, Son of the living God (Mt. 16:16), and decide to become one of his disciples, it's like beginning life all over again. The Greek word used in John 3:16 to describe our new birth can be translated "born again," "born from above," or "born anew." Which translation do you like best? Why?

END

SCHOOL
2

Disciples Learn Together with Jesus

[Jesus] went up the mountain and called to him those whom he wanted, and they came to him. And he appointed twelve, whom he also named apostles, to be with him, and to be sent out to proclaim the message, and to have authority to cast out demons. (Mk. 3:13–15)

In the verses above, Mark describes what it looks like to become a disciple. Jesus calls us. We come to him. In his presence, we learn about God's love and the way God wants us to live. Then Jesus sends us out, giving us power to help others and to tell them about God.

This pattern repeats throughout our lives. Jesus invites us into his presence. Then Jesus commissions us to serve God. Sometimes we resist. Sometimes serving is difficult and things don't work out as we expect. Sometimes we are surprised by how well things go. Always, Jesus calls us to come back to be with him. We go back to Jesus for forgiveness, for healing, for celebration, for encouragement, and for new strength. Jesus helps us grow up. No matter how old we are, in his presence and in his service we are always learning new lessons about God, about ourselves, and about the world around us.

Jesus is our teacher and our guide. We call him Lord, meaning Master, because we yield to him—as would a student to a teacher or a player to a coach. Whether we want to dance, play soccer, operate a computer, or follow Jesus, we have to learn a new set of skills. We can study from a book or in a classroom, but we learn new skills best by practicing them alongside another, more experienced person.

One of the most difficult lessons we learn is how self-centered we are. As newborns, the world revolved around us. If we cried loud enough, somebody would pick us up, give us a hug or something to eat, or change our diaper. Babies are sweet when they're babies. But a part of growing up is learning how, in healthy ways, to overcome our self-centeredness and to put God and other people at the center of our lives.

Learning new skills is often accompanied by the need to learn a new vocabulary. Following Jesus, we discover the meaning of words such as *gospel, sin, atonement, grace, baptism, salvation,* and *sanctification.* These words describe what life is like from God's point of view, the way it really is, and the way it will be with God's help. Our Christian vocabulary helps us describe our experiences and beliefs. Even familiar words, such as *love* and *forgiveness,* take on new depths of meaning in our life with Jesus. *The word* disciple *means "learner, or pupil." We will always be going to school with Jesus.*

TRIP JOURNAL

School

Disciples learn together with Jesus.

> Jesus went up the mountain and called to him those whom he wanted, and they came to him. And he appointed twelve, whom he also named apostles, to be with him, and to be sent out to proclaim the message, and to have authority to cast out demons. (Mk. 3:13–15)

Each Alone

Write some notes below about what you like about school. What do you dislike?

Mentors and Disciples in Pairs

Share what you wrote about your school experiences.

How was following Jesus like going to school for Jesus' disciples? What do you think they liked and disliked? Take some notes here.

What do you think Jesus wanted to teach his disciples? List a few things below.

If you are learning a foreign language, name some of the difficulties. If not, what do you think it must be like to learn a new language? Write your answers here.

The Group in Class

Following Jesus, we learn a new vocabulary. In small groups, look up in dictionaries the words on the next page assigned to you. Put your definitions into everyday language. Each group will appoint a "teacher" to go to the board and write their given words and definitions and give examples.

Sin:

Confession:

Grace:

Forgiveness:

Atonement:

Salvation:

Holy:

Sanctification:

Write a Note to Yourself
What is the most interesting thing you learned about going to school with Jesus?

One of the common ways Jesus' disciples addressed him was by the title "Rabbi," which is the Hebrew word for "teacher."

END

WORK

3

Disciples Get a Job Loving God and Others

"So if I, your Lord and Teacher, have washed your feet, you also ought to wash one another's feet. For I have set you an example, that you also should do as I have done to you." (Jn. 13:14–15)

All four gospel writers tell about the evening before Jesus' crucifixion. Jesus and his disciples shared a last meal together. In their accounts, Matthew, Mark, and Luke emphasize Jesus' request for his disciples to remember him in eating and drinking together. Surprisingly, John doesn't mention the meal. He recalls another way in which, that night, Jesus asked his disciples to remember him. John tells how the disciples' teacher took a towel and a bowl of water, and washed their feet as if he were a servant. When Jesus finished he said, "You also should do as I have done to you" (John 13:15).

Foot washing was a welcomed gesture of hospitality in a dry and dusty climate. By washing his followers' feet (they protested that *they* should be washing *his*), Jesus shows us what working for God looks like. It is stooping to serve others, serving in humility and in love.

But if watching Jesus were not enough, he left a written job description. There are at least two parts. One is called *The Great Commandment* (Mt. 22:34–40). The other is called *The Great Commission* (Mt. 28:19–20). In the first, Jesus commands us to love God and to love our neighbor as ourselves—just as he did. In the second, Jesus commands us to go and make disciples—just as he did.

Loving others and inviting them to follow Jesus is hard work. We need God's help. We need the support of others who are also learning how to do God's work: putting others first, speaking the truth in love, forgiving one another, feeding the hungry, working to right wrongs, loving enemies, and helping strangers feel at home. To do the job, God gives each of us different abilities. Then God leads us to those places where *our skills* and *our joy* help meet people's deepest needs.

Our "job" as Christians is to do well the things we do and, by way of our speech and our actions, to show others how much God loves them.

Trip Journal

Work

Disciples get a job loving God and others.

> "Whoever wishes to become great among you must be your servant…
> For the Son of Man came not to be served but to serve, and to give his
> life a ransom for many." (Mk. 10:43–45)

Each Alone

Below write three words that describe your experience of serving others through
your work today.

What activity are you good at doing? How did you learn to do this? What were
your resources?

Write down the name of your favorite teacher or coach. What qualities make him
or her your favorite? Why do you listen to and obey a favorite teacher or coach?

Mentors and Disciples in Pairs

Share and talk about what you wrote above.

For the disciple: Have you thought about what you want to do as your vocation?
Write down the possibilities and then discuss with your mentor.

For the mentor: In a few words, describe your vocation (how you use God's gifts to
provide for you and your loved ones and the church's mission). Then discuss with
your disciple how your vocation provides opportunities to serve others.

Disciples Job Description

The Great Commandment

"'You shall love the Lord your God with all your heart, and with all your soul, and with all your mind.' This is the greatest and first commandment. And a second is like it: 'You shall love your neighbor as yourself'" (Matthew 22:37–39).

The Great Commission

"Go therefore and make disciples of all nations, baptizing them in the name of the Father and of the Son and of the Holy Spirit, and teaching them to obey everything that I have commanded you" (Matthew 28:19–20a).

Role-play: Interviewing for the Job

Jesus teaches his disciples that no matter what we decide to do to make a living, he has given us another very important job: *to love God and to love others, and to invite others to become disciples of Jesus*. In pairs, disciples and mentors will conduct a job interview. Read the *Disciples Job Description* at left. One person plays the part of interviewer; the other plays the part of interviewee. Ask and answer questions like the following:

✓ Why do you want the job?

✓ What qualifications do you have for the job?

✓ What do you think you will find most difficult in fulfilling this job description?

✓ Who will you ask for help when you need it in this job?

Write one thing you learned about "working" for Jesus:

WALKING IN THE SPIRIT

4

Disciples Experience God's Presence Everywhere

"Just as the branch cannot bear fruit by itself unless it abides in the vine, neither can you unless you abide in me. I am the vine, you are the branches." (Jn. 15:4b–5a)

Very near the end of his life, Jesus told his disciples that he would be leaving them. They didn't understand. They were afraid. They asked a question for all of us: Jesus, how can we do all that you have taught us when you are not here to help us? Jesus answered by pointing to a vineyard where grapes were grown and making a promise. Jesus said that his disciples are like branches. That he is like the vine. "Remain attached to me," Jesus said, "and your lives will produce delicious fruit."

Then Jesus promised to send a helper, the Holy Spirit (Jn. 14:15–16). The Spirit is God's presence bringing forgiveness, understanding, strength, and guidance—not just in church, but in every moment, wherever we are: at home, in the mall, in school, with friends. God's love and help are available to us everywhere.

Two lists are associated with the Holy Spirit. The first is a list of the Spirit's *gifts*, including abilities such as teaching, healing, leading, serving, and giving (see 1 Cor. 12 and 14; Rom. 12:3–8; Eph. 4:11–13). Every Christian is given at least one gift to help us keep the Great Commandment and to fulfill the Great Commission. You could call it the "Great Empowerment." When God asks us to do something, God gives us God's Spirit, the Helper. Together, our various gifts help us create a healthy community in the church.

The second is a list of the Spirit's *fruit*: love, joy, peace, patience, kindness, generosity, faithfulness, gentleness, and self-control (see Galatians 5:22–23). God not only helps us live like Christ; God makes us more Christlike, changing us from the inside out. The fruit of the Spirit isn't a list of attributes that we work on in order to measure up in God's sight. These marks of Christ's character grow in us, like fruit on a vine, as we remain attached to Jesus.

Christians practice skills, such as prayer and reading the Bible, that help us remain attached to Jesus. We call them spiritual disciplines. They help us recognize God's presence. Prayer is the word we use to describe our talking and listening to God. We read the Bible to learn about God's love and will for the world and how God has worked in the lives of people just like us. The Holy Spirit helps us understand what we read. Jesus said: "Just as the branch cannot bear fruit by itself unless it abides in the vine, neither can you unless you abide in me" (Jn. 15:4b). *We cannot live by ourselves the kind of life to which Jesus calls us. Jesus never intended us to. Through the Holy Spirit, God abides in us and we abide in God.*

11

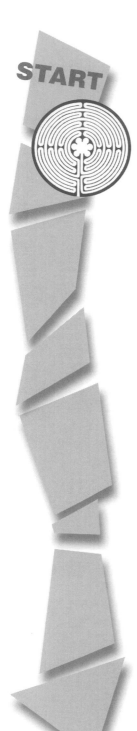

Trip Journal

Walking in the Spirit

Disciples experience God's love and direction.

> "I am the vine, you are the branches." (Jn. 15:5a) —Jesus

Creating sacred space, such as a labyrinth, a sanctuary, or a campfire, can remind disciples that the whole of life is sacred. For centuries, Christians have walked labyrinths as a way to focus their prayer and open their lives to God.

Like a labyrinth, life has many twists and turns. Walking the labyrinth, we can be reminded that God is at work in all the twists and turns to help us live a whole and holy life. Think of a labyrinth as a pilgrimage or a journey. Walking toward the center can be an expression of our purposely turning toward God. Spending time in the center can bring calm in the midst of life's many distractions. The journey outward can help a person recommit to discover God's presence in every twist and turn of everyday live. The labyrinth may look like a maze, but it isn't. It has only one way in and one way out. You cannot get lost.

Each Alone: Walking the Labyrinth

Preparation: Take a moment to invite God to walk the labyrinth with you. If you wish, decide on a prayer or simple phrase to carry with you as you walk, such as "God is love." Be respectful of others as you pass them in the labyrinth.

Inward Journey: Let go of the distractions of everyday life. Ask God to help you release the things that get in the way of your relationship with God. As you walk, open your heart and quiet your mind.

In the Center: Stay as long or as briefly as you like in the middle. Rest in God's grace while praying and listening.

Outward Journey: Ask God to help you prepare to reenter your life with renewed faith, hope, love, and joy. Listen as God may speak to you about your life outside the labyrinth. Just as you let go of the world on the way in, you may think about how you want to share yourself and God's love anew in the world.

After you have walked the labyrinth, record your thoughts and feelings about your experience.

Mentors and Disciples in Pairs: Choose Two

Read Romans 6:3–11 together.

The apostle Paul says that in our baptism two things happen. One, our old selves die and are buried with Jesus, just as he was crucified on the cross. Two, we are raised to live a new life, just as Jesus was resurrected from death. Paul is talking about that place in us that resists doing God's will (our old selves, our sinful selves). Through Jesus and our trust in him, God forgives our sin. The Holy Spirit helps us "walk in newness of life." *Talk about what this means to you.*

Read John 15:1–5 together.

For a branch to survive, it has to remain attached to the vine—twenty-four hours a day, seven days a week. Jesus wants his followers to know that no matter where we are or what time it is, the Holy Spirit is with us to help us think and speak and act like Jesus. Life is not always easy. Sometimes it is very hard. Family members get mad and yell at each other, or worse. Friends abandon us. We don't always do well on tests. We fail to make a team. Yet God promises to be with us in the difficult times. He gives us a helper, the Holy Spirit. *Discuss a time when God has helped you.*

Fruit of the Spirit
Love
Joy
Peace
Patience
Kindness
Generosity
Faithfulness
Gentleness
Self-control

Read John 15:1–5 together.

Using crayons or markers, draw a vine and its branches. Put clusters of grapes on some of the branches. Label some of the grapes with the names of the kind of fruit you would like to produce (Gal 5:22). Draw a branch or two, broken and lying on the ground, representing God's pruning in our lives. Discuss your drawings and how they represent your lives as followers of Jesus.

To Do on Your Own Later

Read 1 Corinthians 9:24–27. When the apostle Paul wrote to the young Christians in Corinth, he reminded them of the Olympic Games, which took place in their city. Paul encourages followers of Jesus to exercise our faith so that we might grow stronger. Name specific ways you exercise: physically (playing sports), mentally (studying for school), and emotionally (learning to share your thoughts and feelings with family and friends). God asks us to exercise spiritually, too. By reading the Bible and praying regularly, we practice to get better. Exercise strengthens us.

END

MEAL TIME

5

Disciples Are Fed at the Lord's Table

While they were eating, Jesus took a loaf of bread, and after blessing it he broke it, gave it to the disciples, and said, "Take, eat, this is my body." Then he took a cup, and after giving thanks he gave it to them, saying, "Drink from it, all of you; for this is my blood of the covenant, which is poured out for many for the forgiveness of sins." (Mt. 26:26–29)

In the New Testament, we read of many occasions when people invited Jesus to dinner. Sometimes he invited himself. Every time something extraordinary happened. A woman's sins were forgiven (Lk. 7:36–50). Five thousand people were fed with five fish and two loaves of bread (Lk. 9:10–17). In one home, Jesus taught that we can be so busy getting ready to eat that we miss the real meal (Lk. 10:38–41). One time a man was healed (Lk. 14:1–6). Another time a despised tax collector promised to give away half of the things he owned and to pay back all that he had stolen from people (Lk. 19:1–10).

One meal stands out above the rest. On the eve of Jesus' crucifixion, he and his disciples shared in the *Seder* (Mt. 26:17–29). During this meal, Jewish people celebrate Passover, the time when God freed their ancestors from harsh slavery in Egypt. They prepare the food that their ancestors were instructed to eat before their long journey of escape into the wilderness. Jesus took the bread on the table and gave it a new meaning. He blessed it, broke it, and gave it to his disciples, saying, "This is my body." He took the cup on the table and passing it to them said, "This is my blood...poured out for many for the forgiveness of sins."

Jesus is saying that through the way he lived and died our sins are forgiven and we are invited into a new relationship with God. Just as God delivered the Jews from slavery in Egypt and gave them a new start, God delivers us from our slavery to sin and gives us a new start. Each time we gather around the Lord's table, we remember Jesus' death, we thank him for pouring out his life for us, we celebrate his presence, and we commit ourselves to serve him.

Whenever Jesus joins us in a meal, amazing things can happen, such as forgiveness, healing, and new life—and not just in church. Our Sunday gathering at the Lord's table is a practice session for the rest of the week. Every day God invites us to life, as if it were a banquet overflowing with all kinds of good things to eat, drink, experience, and share with each other, with strangers, with our enemies even. *God asks us to take the whole of life—the best and the worst that come—and bless it, break it, and share it with others as a precious gift. This is why there is a dinner table at the center of our worship space.*

Trip Journal

The Family Dinner Table

Disciples eat and drink together with Jesus.

"I am the bread of life." (Jn. 6:35)

The tour guide will divide the chores. Some will set the table. Others will serve the meal. Someone will offer a blessing. Everybody will help clean up.

Group Discussion around the Table

Listed below are some of the things we do when we eat together. With the people seated around you, remember and share times when your family did some of these things.

At the family dinner table, and at the Lord's table:

1. We thank God for life, food, and each other.
2. We remember others and their needs.
3. We share what has happened during our day.
4. We listen to each other's stories.
5. We remember the past.
6. We talk about the future.
7. And we eat.

To Read and Think about on Your Own Later

Jesus said, "I am the bread of life" (Jn. 6:35). What do you think Jesus means?

When you eat with others, how can you help make amazing things such as forgiveness, joy, and love happen in their lives?

Throughout the centuries, Christians have used different words to describe their time around the table in worship.

- The *Lord's Supper* or the Lord's *Last Supper* (emphasizing that Christ Jesus is our host at the table and in life; a reminder that this was the last meal he shared with his friends, the disciples, before his arrest, trial, and crucifixion)

- *Communion* (emphasizing how we share together—create a community—with God and each other when we gather around the Lord's table)

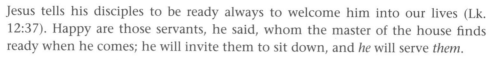

- The *eucharist* (from the Greek language, meaning "thanksgiving," emphasizing our gratitude for Jesus' life, the meaning of his death, and God's gift of new life)

Which description do you like best? Why?

Jesus tells his disciples to be ready always to welcome him into our lives (Lk. 12:37). Happy are those servants, he said, whom the master of the house finds ready when he comes; he will invite them to sit down, and *he* will serve *them*.

What an amazing thing: Jesus welcomes us to his table and then serves us! All along in our life's journey, Jesus nourishes us: through others in their love and care for us; in our study of the Bible; in prayer; at his table in worship; in the beauty and provision of God's good creation; and through the Holy Spirit's presence every day.

END

Disciples Enjoy God's Creation and Their Relationships

And on the seventh day God finished the work that he had done, and he rested on the seventh day from all the work that he had done. (Gen. 2:2)

One day Jesus sent his disciples on their first mission trip to practice what they had learned. It was a very busy time. They accomplished a lot, but when they returned Jesus could see that they were tired (Mk. 6:30–32). So Jesus led them away in a boat to a deserted place for rest and renewal. Even in our need for recreation, Jesus gives us a model to follow. Our work becomes ineffective when we do not take time for rest and play. We begin to take ourselves too seriously. We are not very pleasant to be around. Jesus teaches his disciples that rest and play are essential parts of the rhythm of life.

Even God rests! For six days, God worked. On the seventh day, the Bible tells us, God rested from the labor of creation (Gen. 2:2). We refer to this day of rest as "the seventh day of creation," suggesting that rest is as important a part of creating something as the work involved. Perhaps this is why we call our times of rest and play "recreation."

Just as God enjoyed the fruit of the divine labor on the seventh day, we are invited to relax and play. Because God is still at work in the world, we don't have to take ourselves and our work too seriously. We can slow down and enjoy life's pleasures. Because God loves and forgives us, we can forgive ourselves and others. God's promise of resurrection from death—offering us second chances, new starts, and life everlasting—gives us a sense of playfulness even in life's most discouraging, difficult, and dangerous moments.

There is something to be learned through play. Even in times of unsupervised recreation, children naturally come up with rules. This is because rules can be a gift. Good rules bring structure and meaning to our play. Keeping the rules is a way to honor each other and bring God's justice to the world. The Ten Commandments are God's gift, given to help us be good stewards of creation, to enjoy life, and to see that everyone has a chance to enjoy life too.

We are invited to relax in our relationship with Jesus. Following Jesus can be fun.

Trip Journal

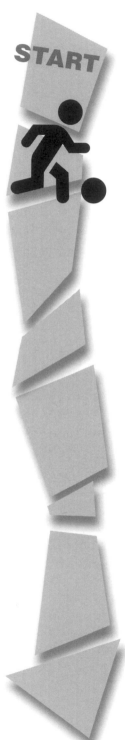

Play

Disciples enjoy God's creation and their relationships.

> "[Jesus] said to them, 'Come away to a deserted place all by yourselves and rest a while'" (Mk. 6:31).

Time to play! After a game or two, your tour guide will lead you in group conversation.

Group Discussion (Take some notes here.)

Why are rest and play important to us as human beings—so important that God requires us to observe a day of rest each week?

What does the phrase "play fair" mean? Why is playing fair so important?

Can you think of a single game that doesn't have any rules? What would happen if there weren't any rules, any boundaries, in our games?

The Bible has a word for breaking the rules: *sin*. The Bible says that all human beings are sinners. Why do we have such a hard time keeping God's rules?

Mentors and Disciples in Pairs

Read the modern paraphrase of the Ten Commandments printed on the next page. Discuss which commandments you don't understand, which are easy for you to follow, and which are difficult for you to follow. (You can look up the original commandments in Ex. 20:1–17.)

How do rules in the games we play compare to the Ten Commandments?

In what ways do we experience more freedom and joy in having rules than in our not having any rules to live by?

Read Micah 6:6–8. Then one of you read the following.

God called the prophet Micah to speak to God's people during a time when ancient Israel's political and spiritual leaders were thinking only about themselves. Good people were outwardly observing the religious customs and traditions of their day, but they weren't caring for the people and the groups who were in need: widows and orphans, the sick and hungry, aliens and the poor. Micah reminded them that God is more interested in our doing the right thing, doing the kind thing, and walking in humility with God.

What does the word *justice* mean?

The Ten Commandments in Rhyme

   I. Above all else love God alone,
  II. Bow down to neither wood nor stone.
 III. God's name, refuse to take in vain;
 IV. The Sabbath rest with care maintain.
  V. Respect your parents all your days;
 VI. Hold sacred human life always.
VII. Be loyal to your chosen mate;
VIII. Steal nothing, neither small nor great.
 IX. Report, with truth, your neighbor's deed;
  X. And rid your mind of selfish greed.

from McGuffey's Reader

Think about the games you played. How is "playing fair" like *doing justice*?

Can you name a place in the world where people are suffering injustice?

What does Micah mean when he calls us to walk humbly with God? What does humility have to do with justice and kindness?

To Read on Your Own Later

God came up with the Ten Commandments because God loves us and is concerned about how we live our everyday lives. God wants us to live in ways that bring fullness, pleasure, safety, and a sense of community. Keeping the rules brings a joy-filled life to us and to others around us. Breaking the rules leads to death— emotionally, spiritually, and physically. Knowing that we are all rule-breakers makes God's unconditional love for us all the more amazing.

END

DEATH AND RESURRECTION
7

Disciples Face Death with Courage and Hope

Then Jesus said to [his disciples], "Do not be afraid; go and tell my brothers to go to Galilee; there they will see me." (Mt. 28:10)

Before the church describes resurrection as a spiritual experience or a religious belief, it is first of all a universal human experience: the gift of God's mercy, forgiveness, and power for new life. By God's grace, resurrection happens to everyone and everything—from the healing of broken bones and broken hearts to the healing of the environment and the mending of relationships between nations.

In the beginning, God created resurrection and wove it into the fabric of life First comes life; then comes death; then comes rebirth—in this life as well as the next.

This is not to diminish the mystery of Jesus' Easter morning appearances or our anticipation of the resurrection morning still to come—when, as John describes in his vision, God will make "all things new" (Rev. 21:5). Nor does this truth reduce the pain we experience when a loved one dies or a cherished hope goes unrealized. Death is dark and difficult. But when the church's attention is focused only on the life yet to come, we miss the new life that is springing up, resurrection-like, all around and in us—even in the midst of the many sad endings we experience.

We also miss a startling truth. The disciples understood that Jesus' resurrection was not an exception to the rule, but a dramatic demonstration of God's ordinary way in the world. They embraced resurrection as a concrete reality and practiced it daily. Old hurts were healed. Broken relationships were mended. Physical illnesses were cured. People turned from their sins and lived lives of integrity and faith. The walls dividing people and cultures gave way to new ways of being together.

As the women ran from the empty tomb, the risen Christ Jesus greeted them and said, "Do not be afraid; go and tell my brothers to go to Galilee; there they will see me" (Mt. 28:10). Galilee was home for the disciples, the land where they first met and served with Jesus. Galilee represents the places of our everyday lives, where Jesus walks beside us and brings us from death to new life again and again.

Jesus taught us to pray, "Your kingdom come. / Your will be done, / on earth as it is in heaven" (Mt. 6:10). Wherever we practice resurrection, the kingdom has come. God's will is for new life—in this life as well as the next.

Trip Journal

Death and Resurrection

Disciples face death with courage and hope.

> "He has been raised from the dead, and indeed he is going ahead of you to Galilee; there you will see him." (Mt. 28:7)

Each Alone

The group travels to a funeral home where the conversation turns to death and resurrection. Pay attention to your feelings as you explore the funeral home and hear what is said.

Our feelings about death are powerful. Jot down some notes here about what you are feeling, any questions you may want to ask, and what you will remember about this place.

Do you fear death? Why or why not?

Mentors and Disciples in Pairs

Discuss what you wrote.

Read the following together and talk about it.

Most of us think about death and resurrection as experiences that will come sometime in the distant future. However, the Bible teaches that experiences of death and resurrection are also a part of our everyday lives. Can you think of experiences of "death and resurrection" in your life? For example, maybe you moved to a new town, away from friends, and yet you made new friends and had new opportunities through the move. Or maybe you were an only child until a sibling came along and took away your "privileged" status. In some part of your life, maybe you are experiencing a kind of death or ending right now and haven't yet experienced a resurrection. Talk about these experiences together.

As time allows, pick one or two of the following.

Name a time when you blew it. What happened? What did it take on your part to recover from this time? What did others do to help you start over?

Jesus said, "I am the resurrection and the life. Those who believe in me, even though they die, will live, and everyone who lives and believes in me will never die" (Jn. 11:25–26). *Stop and talk about what this means to each of you.*

Jesus was talking about a quality of life that comes from our believing that, in every kind of death we experience, God is at work to bring hope and healing, second chances, and new life. We enter into this quality of life and the confidence and joy it brings—what Jesus calls eternal life—when we put our trust in Jesus and work with him to bring new life out of the old. *Describe a time when you have experienced this kind of eternal life.*

Maybe you have a friend who is thinking about committing suicide (taking his or her own life). As a friend, you have two responsibilities. First, you can share with your friend that you have learned about how God can help make things better in this life. This is a part of what it means to believe in resurrection here and now. When we reach out and ask for the help of God and others, tomorrow can be better.

Second, even if you have promised your friend not to tell, this is one promise it is okay to break. Your friend may be mad at you for a time, but telling a responsible adult is one way you can help bring resurrection to your friend in this life.

To Read on Your Own Later

God has written resurrection from death into every part of life, even in snowflakes. When a snowflake melts, it may seem to disappear. But it joins a stream somewhere, goes to a river, enters the ocean and, by way of evaporation, has the chance to become a snowflake again. What other signs of death and resurrection do you see in the world?

Do you think an empty tomb representing new life would be the better symbol of the Christian faith than a cross representing death? Why do you think the church has chosen a cross to represent our faith?

END

CHURCH

8

Disciples Gather to Celebrate and Prepare

Now you are the body of Christ and individually members of it. (1 Cor. 12:27)

When we decide to follow Jesus, we become a part of his community, the Church, because God knows we need each other. Living a Christlike life is not easy. Jesus' followers help each other by growing up together in our new life—learning, working, eating, playing, and practicing our faith together. We share each other's joys when things go well. We forgive each other when we fail. We serve the world together. This is what Jesus was doing when he gathered the twelve and put them through hands-on training for three years. They were learning God's ways. Jesus was turning his followers into servants like himself, teaching them to bring God's help and hope to others, and showing them how to live together loving God, serving others, and changing lives.

All around the world in Jesus' name, the Church still gathers followers, turning them into servants and equipping them to carry out God's mission. Together, as the apostle Paul says, the church is the body of Christ and each of us members of it (Rom. 12:4–5). In spite of our sinful divisions, misunderstandings, and shortcomings as Christians, the Church is called to be a vessel of God's compassion and power—as Jesus was.

When we forget our high calling—to be representatives of God's love and presence—church activities become religious busy-work that distracts us from seeing God and serving others. We end up talking about *going* to church (and sometimes dreading it) rather than *being* the Church, God's representatives in the world.

So, everything we do together inside the church building is designed to help us serve God outside the building. At the door, we welcome strangers. In the sanctuary, we praise God, come clean through confession and forgiveness, and are nourished at the Lord's table. In classrooms, we read and discuss the Bible to find direction and inspiration. In places of fellowship, we enjoy one another's company and express our needs and hopes in prayer. In small groups, we share our resources to support the church's life and we plan our church's mission in the world.

In every generation, people have decided to follow Jesus, not first of all because of what Christians do in the church, but because of what participation in the church does to Christians. Our participation in the body of Christ changes us. *Through sharing our experiences of God's grace, we become gracious people who live lives of faith, hope, and love. Through our example, others will want to follow Jesus.*

Trip Journal

Church

Disciples gather to celebrate and prepare.

> "Now you are the body of Christ and individually members of it."
> (1 Cor. 12:27)

We end our *Tour of Life* in the church building. It's the place where the community of God, God's family, meets to celebrate God's love, heal our wounds, and prepare ourselves to be more faithful disciples of Jesus.

Mentors and Disciples in Pairs

Have some fun making a list of the names of the different rooms in your church building and describing how each helps you understand and experience the Great Commission and the Great Commandment. Write down as many of the spaces as you can.

What do you like about church? What do you dislike?

Mentor, share with your disciple what it means to you to be a part of the church.

- How is the community of believers important to you?

- What does it mean for Jesus to be your Lord and Savior?

- In what programs or ministries do you participate that help you grow as a disciple?

- How do you serve here in the church? In the world?

Read together.

Disciple, what is the next stop on *your* "Tour of Life"? You get to decide.

We begin our life of discipleship by affirming our trust in Jesus. In some churches, this happens when we're ready to be baptized. In other churches, if we were baptized when we were children, this happens when we're ready to be confirmed.

In either case, you'll be asked to decide for yourself whether you want to become a follower of Jesus. It's an important decision. No one wants to rush you. Becoming a disciple of Christ is a great adventure—full of danger, risk, reward, and great joy!

You may want more time to think and pray and talk to others about your decision. Or you may be ready to say, "Yes." You decide.

Read the following prayer and think about what you might like to add to it. Then pray together.
"Dear God, thank you for our time together on this Tour of Life. *(Take a moment to add anything you would like to pray here.)* In Jesus' name, amen."

Back Together as a Group

As pairs finish their discussions, your tour guide will call the group together to celebrate your time together and close the tour.

Later, on Your Own

There may be people in your family and among your friends who would like to hear about your *Tour of Life* experience. Think about who they might be, and list their names here.

Find some time to talk with your friends and family. Bring your Trip Journal entries and tell them what you would like them to know.

END

Packing Instructions
for Tour Guide

TOUR PREPARATION

Overview of *Tour of Life*

Tour of Life is an active/interactive learning experience designed to prepare older children and youth for baptism or confirmation. During *Tour of Life,* candidates for baptism or confirmation are paired with a mentor and led as a group on a journey through the seasons of life. In a variety of settings—a hospital's birthing center, a school classroom, a labyrinth, the church's sanctuary, a funeral home, and more—disciples and mentors explore the intersections of Christian discipleship and everyday life.

Throughout the tour, participants are encouraged to see Jesus' way of life as the deepest and most fulfilling of many choices offered in the world. Youth participate with enthusiasm as they begin to get the big picture. Adult mentors have reported receiving as much new insight as the youth.

Tour of Life may be used to enhance more traditional models of preparation for confirmation and baptism or as a stand-alone experience in the following ways:

- In a one- or two-day retreat
- Over several weeks, one experience a week

If you choose the retreat format, it is recommended that the tour be designed to start one evening and end the next day. One of the advantages of a more condensed time together is that participants get a sweeping overview of the Christian life. On the other hand, one of the advantages of using the material over several weeks is that its themes may be explored in more depth and details of the tour stop experiences are more likely to be savored if not experienced en masse.

In addition to use with youth, *Tour of Life* has also been used effectively by young adults in a retreat setting. Each participant receives a copy of *Tour of Life.* The material disciples and mentors use from one destination to the next includes:

- A brief, biblical overview of the theme at each tour stop
- Scriptures, activities, and discussion starters related to each stop

This workbook also includes "Guide Tips" (see page 43), essential suggestions for leading the group at each destination. For a more thorough overview, read the Introduction and review the Itinerary.

Definitions and Expectations

Tour Guide: staff person or trusted member of the church family who is willing to volunteer for this role.

The tour guide's responsibilities include at least the following:

- Be thoroughly familiar with the entire *Tour of Life* manual.

- Be responsible for ensuring that all the pre-tour arrangements are completed.

- Schedule and announce the event long in advance.

- Recruit and pair mentors and disciples.

- Communicate with parents and guardians regarding tour details.

- Lead the tour group through the experience, introducing each tour stop by reading the related introductory material (or sharing it in one's own words), serving as time-keeper at each stop, and keeping the group on schedule.

Mentor: person of mature faith and familiarity with the congregation.

A mentor's responsibilities include the following:

- Participate in the entire tour.

- Mentor one candidate and accompany said candidate through the entire tour.

- Be in a learning mode during the tour, taking notes in the Trip Journal as example and encouragement to the disciple.

- Bring a Bible and pencil to each session, and baby picture to the first session.

Disciple: an older child or youth who has indicated an interest in being baptized, being confirmed, or learning more about the Christian faith.

A disciple is expected to

- Participate in and complete the entire tour

- Be a cooperative and willing partner with others in the group

- Bring a Bible and pencil to each session, and baby picture to the first session

Notes for the Tour Guide

Preacher Fred Craddock suggests that we take a journey three times: in our anticipation and preparation; in the adventure itself; and in our memory of it. Prepare well and the tour will create many wonderful memories. Why not invite a small team of persons to help you prepare for the adventure? *One of the most crucial elements of preparation is contacting staff at each of the tour destinations well in advance to make arrangements for the group's visits.*

Tour of Life has been created so that mentors, like disciples, may experience the tour without preparation. However, a brief meeting of mentors could be scheduled to include a time of prayer, an overview of the experience, and a quick walk through the Trip Journal. It's recommended that the Trip Journals then be collected so that mentors may read and, thus, experience the tour, like their disciples, as something new and unexpected.

Each tour stop has four components.

1. The site. It is difficult to underestimate the importance of the group's gathering at each site. The tour destinations are an indispensable part of the experience.
2. An introduction. The tour guide should read a brief overview of the biblical background and theological importance of each site. The "theme statement" of each session (in italics at beginning of Itinerary sections) printed in italics, may be repeated at the end of each stop.
3. "Trip Journal" pages. Mentors and disciples are encouraged to complete the exercises and take notes in their Trip Journals.
4. "Guide Tips." At the end of this book, there are specific suggestions and a list of needed materials to help the tour guide lead the experience at each stop.

Be encouraged to use the material in any way that will be helpful to the participants and your congregation. Experiment, making it your own experience.

You may ask, "Really, how long does the tour take?" Really, you can conduct a tour in twelve hours, including snacks, the meal, bathroom breaks and travel time. Start early one day and you can be done by dinner. Turn the experience into an overnight retreat: include two stops the first evening and, by starting early the next morning, you can conclude by four o'clock. Expect some sessions to last forty-five minutes. A couple may last an hour and fifteen minutes. You decide the length of time you want to spend in the service project. An hour and a half of work is usually sufficient. Disciples will be surprised by how much the group can accomplish together in this amount of time.

You will have to move the group along. Try to schedule stops that don't take a long drive time. However, part of the fun and energy—and a time when a lot of good conversation takes place—is moving quickly and safely from destination to destination. Have you ever been on a trip when you got to spend all the time you wanted in all the places you wanted? Or are you usually left wanting to return to certain sites to see them more closely? Similarly, *Tour of Life* is an exciting overview of the Christian life, not a detailed, step-by-step walk through the whole of it.

As you prepare for the tour, think about how this experience fits and can enhance your congregation's traditions for preparing children and youth for an active life in and through the church. Put some thought into how you will want to draw the *Tour of Life* experience to a close. Will you ask your mentors to stay in touch with their disciples over the next twelve months? If so, explain this as a part of a mentor's responsibilities when you recruit them. On page 41 there are suggestions for how to bring the experience to a close.

A week or so before the tour, send a letter to parents/guardians that includes at least the following: a brief overview of the tour; a list of the items disciples may need (such as a Bible, baby picture, and work clothes and tools for the service project); and a schedule of the tour with details about when and where disciples are to appear for the first stop and when and where they are to be picked up when the tour ends.

Three More Things (Don't Skip These!)

Pray.

Bathe both the tour preparation and the tour experience in prayer. Pray for God's wisdom, discernment and direction as you plan. Pray for the candidates who will participate. Pray that the mentors will both give and grow through the experience. Ask others to pray with you. Ask the entire congregation to pray for those experiencing *Tour of Life*. During the tour, model a life of prayer by including God in the conversation in at least two ways:

- Pause occasionally and spontaneously for prayer. A few times, prayer is specifically called for. But pray any time you and others feel led.

- When you are beginning or concluding an especially sensitive time of sharing, verbally acknowledge to the group that God has been, and will be, a part of the conversation, because God is always with us.

Relax.

Discipleship is lifelong adventure. We're all on our way together. Even professional tour guides can't answer all the questions they're asked. Don't worry about disciples "getting it." They'll grow through this experience—because it is powerful, because you care, and, most of all, because God is at work in their lives.

Be at peace.

Have you ever taken a tour or vacation during which plans had to be changed and the unexpected, maybe even unwelcome change, ended up being one of the most formative experiences? Be open to the unexpected. Be at peace in Christ.

TOUR GUIDE TIPS

Guide Tips: New Birth

Materials needed for this session:

One *Tour of Life* copy for each mentor and disciple

Poster board and removable tape to mount baby pictures

Extra Bibles and pencils

1. If it is not possible to include a hospital's birthing center on the tour, ask a family with a newborn if the group can briefly visit. Then return to the church or go on to the second stop to work on the New Birth activities in the Trip Journal.

2. Be at the hospital early to welcome participants. Introduce disciples to their mentors. Gather and lightly tape the baby pictures of mentors and disciples on poster board and let participants try to match the pictures with names. Don't reveal the matches yet.

3. When everyone has arrived, ask God to help the group have a fun time together as they discover what it means to be Jesus' followers. Lead the group to the hospital's birthing center. Invite participants to look at the babies through the observation window. Invite comments from the group about what they're observing.

4. Retreat to a corner in the hospital's cafeteria or a classroom for a snack. Pass out the *Tour of Life* books. Invite participants each to write his or her name on the front cover and the name of this first stop at the top of the stop's Trip Journal page.

5. Begin by reading (or sharing in your own words) the introductory material. At this first stop, you may want to talk briefly about the importance of conversation (listening as well as talking) and how mentors as well as disciples are sharing the journey and learning together.

6. Serve as the leader of group dynamics and timekeeper as the group works through the Trip Journals' activities.

7. When most of the pairs have completed their work, let each point to his or her baby picture. Call attention to the clothes in which parents dressed their children for the pictures. Remind the group that according to the letter to the Colossians, Christ wants to clothe us with special qualities of life—the qualities of his life. Read Colossians 3:12. Ask if any of the pairs would share something from their conversation about this passage.

8. Before the group leaves for the next destination, read the summary statement for this first stop (or share it in your own words). *The summary statement for each stop is the last sentence or section of the introductory material of the tour destination and will always be highlighted in italics.*

9. If you have more time, spend a few moments pointing to scriptural images of "journey": the call of Abraham and Sarah; the Israelites on their way from a life of slavery in Egypt to a life of freedom that led through a wilderness of accountability; Jesus on his way from Galilee to Jerusalem and the cross that

awaited him outside of that city's gates. All of life is a journey, involving adventure and risk. Explain the concept of *Tour of Life,* how mentors and disciples are setting out on an adventure together to learn how God's love and guidance is available to us throughout our lives, and how each stop along the way represents a part of our lives.

Guide Tips: School

Materials needed for this session:

Dictionaries (one for each pair)

Extra Bibles

Extra pencils

1. When participants are gathered in the school's foreign language classroom, invite the teacher to welcome them in the language he or she teaches and then to translate. Point to foreign language words and displays posted on the classroom walls and invite participants to try to translate.

2. Continue by reading (or sharing in your own words) the introductory material.

3. Before mentors and disciples are invited to begin the exercise in their Trip Journals, remind mentors and disciples about the importance of everyone sharing in the tour—speaking, asking questions, and listening well to others.

4. Invite participants to write the name of this stop at the top of their Trip Journal pages.

5. Serve as the leader of group dynamics and timekeeper as the group works through the Tour Journal activities.

6. When the group is ready, go over the instructions in the Trip Journal for studying the words that express and shape our understanding of God and what it means to be human. Organize the groups, distribute the dictionaries, and move the group along in its work, especially as each "teacher" goes to the board and shares a definition. Encourage everyone to record each definition in their Trip Journals.

7. While it is still early in the tour, be aware of any relationships between mentors and disciples that may need encouragement or intervention.

8. Before participants finish their Trip Journal pages and prepare to leave the school, remind mentors and disciples to write some notes about the most interesting thing each learned about going to school with Jesus.

9. Before the group leaves for the next destination, read the summary statement for this stop. *The summary statement for each destination is the last sentence or section of the introductory material for the tour destination and will always be highlighted in italics.*

Guide Tips: Work

1. When participants arrive at the service project site, work with those in charge to help participants understand their assignments and to get them started.
2. Encourage participants to enjoy their time together helping others.
3. Once the assignment is completed, gather the group on the site and invite their questions and feedback on the experience.
4. Invite participants to write the name of this stop at the top of their Tour Journal pages.
5. Continue by reading (preferably sharing in your own words and out of your own experiences) the introductory material.
6. Serve as the leader of group dynamics and the timekeeper as the group works through the Tour Journal activities.
7. When the group is ready, explain the "job interview" experience, go over the instructions in the Trip Journal, and move them along in the assignment.
8. When most interviews have been completed, encourage a few to share their experiences.
9. Before the group leaves for the next destination, you may read the summary statement for this destination. *The summary statement for each destination is the last sentence or section of the introductory material for the tour destination and will always be highlighted in italics.*

Materials needed for this session:

Tools needed for the service project (extra work gloves?)

Guide Tips: Walking in the Spirit

Materials needed for this session:

A labyrinth

Paper and crayons or markers

1. If your congregation does not have a labyrinth, there may be a neighboring faith community that would welcome you to experience theirs. Or, through a search on the Web, you can find plans for creating a simple labyrinth with masking tape, as well as companies that sell labyrinths printed on canvas.

2. Begin the stop by inviting participants to write the name of this stop on the top of their Trip Journal pages. Share the introductory material.

3. Many participants may not have experienced walking a labyrinth. Read aloud the description of a labyrinth and suggestions for walking the labyrinth from the Trip Journal. Welcome questions. Without lowering participants' expectations, explain that everyone has a different experience when they walk a labyrinth—from deeply moving to relaxing to "no big deal." Encourage the group to be open to God's Spirit. Ask someone to pray before the group begins.

4. More than one participant can walk the labyrinth at the same time. Depending on the labyrinth's size, as many as seven or eight can walk it at once. Put a minute between the start of each participant. Mentors and disciples walk the labyrinth alone, not as pairs.

5. As disciples and mentors wait their turns to walk—and after the earliest walkers complete the labyrinth—invite them to begin one or two of the activities in their Trip Journals.

6. After everyone has completed the labyrinth, take time to debrief them about the experience. Some may want to share.

7. Before you leave for the next stop on the tour, you may read the summary statement. *The summary statement is the last sentence or section of the introductory material of the tour destination and will always be italicized.*

Guide Tips: Meal Time

1. Perhaps you will have arranged for a group in your church that will have prepared the meal.

2. When participants arrive at the dinner site, divide them into teams (everybody participates). Assign mentors to lead different teams to:
   a. Set the table
   b. Prepare the meal (if necessary for the sake of time, the meal could already be prepared—or maybe you will have ordered pizza)
   c. Serve the meal
   d. Prepare and offer a prayer

Materials needed for this session:
A light lunch and tableware

3. Everybody helps cleaning up after the meal. If possible, serve the meal from the communion table. If the group is small, sit around the table to eat. If the group is larger, sit on the floor as near to the communion table as possible.

4. By now, mentors and disciples should be more relaxed in their relationships. Still, be aware of any relationship that may need encouragement or intervention.

5. As the group shares dinner together, contribute to the conversation around the table.

6. At some point, call for the group's attention. Invite participants to write the name of this tour stop at the top of their Trip Journal pages. Continue by reading (or sharing in your own words and out of your own experiences) the introductory material.

7. Clean up quickly and thoroughly.

8. Before the group leaves for the next destination, you may read the summary statement for this destination and close with a prayer thanking God for mealtimes and all the ways he nourishes the world. *The summary statement for each destination is the last sentence or section of the introductory material of the tour destination and will always be highlighted in italics.*

Guide Tips: Play

Materials needed for this session:

Any resources for the games

1. You can organize rowdy games at any outdoor site. Here's another thought. Since the group will have just finished eating around the Lord's table, why not plan to play in the sanctuary? You may have to get permission from the church's leadership, but explain how wonderful it is that our young people are discovering that God invites us to play as well as pray in God's presence!

2. Lead a couple of games to begin this session. Ensure that the games call for physical energy, are not too competitive, and that everyone participates in some way. Clearly explain the rules of the game and emphasize the importance of keeping the rules. Should someone not be able to participate physically, appoint that person as the timekeeper or the one to whom players address their questions about the game.

3. Invite participants to write the name of this stop on the top of their Trip Journal pages.

4. Share the introductory material. Depending on time constraints, lead discussion on any of the questions that are printed near the top of the Trip Journal pages for this tour destination.

5. Reorganize the group into mentor/disciple pairs for their activities. Remind participants to jot down notes and reflections in their Trip Journals for future recollection.

6. Before the group leaves for the next destination, you may read the summary statement for this destination. *The summary statement for each destination is the last sentence or section of the introductory material of the tour destination and will always be highlighted in italics.*

Guide Tips: Death and Resurrection

1. For some, this may be the tour's most emotional experience. Be sensitive to participants' feelings and questions and the possibility that a few may have had a recent experience of the death of someone close.

2. Gather in the facility's chapel.

3. Ask the facility's host to welcome the group and briefly speak about the role of a funeral home. Most are well-prepared to visit with children and youth about death and dying.

4. Continue by inviting participants to write the name of this stop on the top of their Trip Journal pages.

5. Share the introductory material.

6. The emphasis in this visit is on the power and joy of God to bring resurrection in the midst of death. You may preface the introductory material affirming that the experience of resurrection is not just God's way to get people into heaven in the hereafter. It is also one of God's ways of imparting the joy, the power, and the peace of Jesus and the experience of heaven here and now. God is in the business of rolling away the stones and emptying the tombs in our lives.

7. The host might be asked to give a brief tour of the facility—including, for example, the casket selection room. For youth who have never been in a funeral home, this experience can be quite helpful. It takes away some of the mystery of a funeral home, generates many helpful questions, and prepares disciples for a time when they will attend a funeral. Before the tour of the facility, if any participants do not want to participate, then give them permission to skip this part. Generally, few youth actually decide to sit it out, but be sensitive with those who may not want to see the caskets (leave a mentor with them).

8. Instruct mentors and disciples to get through as much of the Tour Journal material as possible.

9. Before the group leaves for the next destination, read the summary statement for this stop and close with a prayer thanking God for bringing new life and second chances out of all the dead ends and deaths we experience. *The summary statement for each destination is the last sentence or section of the introductory material of the tour destination and will always be highlighted in italics.*

Materials needed for this session:

None

Guide Tips: Church

1. This, the last stop on the tour, will take some thought as you decide how to share your congregation's particular understandings and practices of baptism or confirmation, and how to celebrate and close the tour. See the "Closing Notes" on the next page.

2. Gather participants in a familiar place of fellowship. Invite the group to write the name of this stop on the top of their Trip Journal pages. Share the introductory material.

3. Invite mentors and disciples to complete their assignment together in pairs.

4. Regather the group for instructions about next steps toward baptism or confirmation and a closing celebration.

CLOSING NOTES

Here are several suggestions for how to bring *Tour of Life* to a close. Feel free to come up with your own.

1. Describe and answer questions about the practice of baptism/confirmation in your church's tradition. Prepare candidates for the particulars of this experience. If you have definite plans for a service of confirmation or baptism, prepare a letter with details that disciples can take home. Be sensitive to the reality that some disciples may not be ready to make a decision.

2. Close with worship. If you have prepared a liturgy, invite disciples and mentors to share in its leadership. Invite each participant to share a single word or phrase that describes his or her experience of the tour. Perhaps you will include a service of foot-washing. It's a powerful experience for both mentors and disciples for a mentor to wash the disciple's feet.

3. Provide each mentor with a gift to give to his or her disciple (perhaps a cross or a Bible). If mentors are expected to speak about their disciples—to offer his or her disciple a blessing, for example—alert mentors at the beginning of this day's activities.

4. Ask two or three mentors to be prepared to talk briefly about their experiences of the church as young people and how, then and now, the community of the church helps them live as followers of Jesus in their everyday lives.

5. Do you want to invite families to share in this closing experience?

6. Remind the group of the difference between a casual trip and a pilgrimage. Speak of the elements of a spiritual journey: danger, adventure, risk, and reward.

7. Don't fail to remind participants (and yourself) just how large and generous and unconditional and everlasting is God's grace! Read Romans 8:38–39.

Your kingdom come, Lord, your will be done on earth.

Tour of Life helps young disciples and their mentors explore connections between the church's truths and their everyday experiences. This book can be used as the sole resource for baptism/confirmation preparation or as an enhancement to existing programs. Whether they experience *Tour of Life* over several weeks or all in an exciting weekend, participants are drawn into a deeper faith as they encounter God's hand at work in all stages of their lives.

"In the past few decades, Christians have been good at making believers but not as good at forming disciples. Spiritual formation is an endangered art, and if we aren't careful, we end up with a spirituality that's a mile long and an inch deep. Jeff Wright has created a wonderful resource here to grow up a new generation of Christians who see that our faith is not just a way of believing, but a way of living."

■ *Shane Claiborne, author, activist (www.thesimpleway.org)*

"More and more of us are seeing the need for a reinvigorated process of catechesis—a process that reflects our changing cultural context, good learning theory, and sound theological grounding. Thank God for Jeff Wright and this contribution—a journey-based, experientially-driven, team-oriented, Christ-centered, field-tested approach to confirmation or baptism preparation. It's well-written, clear, and eminently usable. I look forward to hearing stories of its positive impact in forming disciples among new generations."

■ *Brian McLaren, author/speaker (brianmclaren.net)*

"In a culture where our rituals have been simplified and distilled down to a point of near impotence, *Tour of Life* offers an opportunity for churches to breathe new life into the central spiritual act of baptism. With concrete and understandable steps laid out in plain language, congregations can guide seekers through physical, intellectual, emotional, and spiritual exercises, all of which lead to an enriched, indelible understanding of what it means to become a lifelong follower of Christ."

■ *Amy and Christian Piatt, Milagro Christian Church,*
Pueblo, Colorado (milagrocc.org)

JEFF WRIGHT is pastor of Heart of the Rockies Christian Church (Disciples of Christ) in Fort Collins, Colorado. He received his M.Div. from Princeton Theological Seminary and has used the *Tour of Life* experience for several years in his congregational ministry.

CHALICE PRESS

ISBN 978-0-827236-61-5

JEFF WRIGHT

TOUR of LIFE

A Baptism and Confirmation Journey

FAMILY

SCHOOL